STANDARD
LOAN

ENGLISH FOR JOURNALISTS

UNLESS RECALLED BY ANOTHER READER
THIS ITEM MAY BE BORROWED FOR
FOUR WEEKS

To renew, telephone:
01243 816089 (Bishop Otter)
01243 816099 (Bognor Regis)

ENGLISH FOR JOURNALISTS

Wynford Hicks

London and New York

First published 1993
by Routledge
11 New Fetter Lane, London EC4P 4EE

Simultaneously published in the USA and Canada
by Routledge
29 West 35th Street, New York, NY 10001

Reprinted 1994, 1995

© 1993 Wynford Hicks

Typeset in Times and Helvetica, Linotronic 300
by Florencetype Ltd, Kewstoke, Avon
Printed and bound in Great Britain by
TJ Press (Padstow) Ltd, Cornwall

British Library Cataloguing in Publication Data
A catalogue record for this book is available from the
British Library

Library of Congress Cataloguing in Publication Data
A catalogue record for this book is available from the
Library of Congress

ISBN 0-415-09493-3

CONTENTS

ACKNOWLEDGEMENTS

I would like to thank Philip Marsh, founder of PMA Training, for giving me the idea for this book, although it has taken me a long time to write it, and the Wolverhampton *Express and Star* for permission to use material first published in *A Journalist's Guide to the Use of English* by the late Ted Bottomley and Anthony Loftus (1971). This book owes much to theirs, now out of print.

I would like to thank my colleagues – students, trainee journalists and fellow tutors – for their comments and suggestions. Particular thanks to Harriett Gilbert and Harold Frayman for reading the book in typescript and David Simmonds of Simmonds, the Fleet Street booksellers, for helping me compile the section on further reading.

HOW TO USE THIS BOOK

You can, of course, begin the book at the beginning and read it straight through. It is planned to lead you in logical order from the basic rules of English to suggestions on style and vocabulary.

But if you have a particular interest – for example, in punctuation – turn to the chapter that covers it and read that first. You may come across an unfamiliar term, such as 'preposition': use the index to find out where the term is explained. In fact, it is covered in the chapter 'Grammar: the rules'.

If you want advice on a particular point – for example, use of the word 'hopefully' – instead of reading all the chapters where it might be covered, begin with the index. In fact, 'hopefully' is covered in 'Grammar: mistakes and confusions'.

CHAPTER 1

THE USE OF ENGLISH

English is one of the most flexible and expressive languages in the world. Its immense vocabulary provides for the precise and persuasive communication of ideas. It is a language of subtle verbal inflections, which enable the writer to project mood and emotion, to formulate thought and principle with clarity and impact. It is a language made for, and by, poets, playwrights and philosophers. And it is a reporter's language in which graphic words can be used to tell a story in vivid detail.

But the very richness of English makes it difficult to use well. If there are always so many ways of saying something, how can you be sure you have chosen the right one? For example, should you write in formal English or as you speak? Should you use long, impressive phrases or short, expressive ones? And what about imported words, whether from a foreign language or American?

English began as a combination of Anglo-Saxon and French with a strong dose of Latin, and as it spread, developed a series of dialects – American, Australian, West Indian and so on. Today the strongest influence on the way we speak and write is undoubtedly American. In the global village of satellites and computers it is in American rather than English that nation speaks unto nation.

But that is no reason why we in Britain should say 'off and running' instead of 'up and running', 'around 50' instead of 'about 50', 'meet up with' instead of 'meet' – or why we should 'wash up' before we eat rather than afterwards or start wearing our 'vests' over rather than under our shirts. Above all, we should avoid the ugly American jargon of modern warfare, marketing and computerbabble.

The best advice to a journalist is: write for your reader. You should use a clear form of English, avoiding jargon, slang, pomposity, academic complexity, obscurity . . .

Different publications have different readers so you should apply common sense. A broadsheet newspaper will use longer words than a tabloid; a trade magazine will be more formal than a women's magazine; a specialist computer magazine can hardly avoid some jargon. But the general principles of good writing apply to all publications.

1

This book takes as a premise that standard English is a useful means of communication and that it is essential for journalists to learn and remember the rules of grammar, spelling and punctuation. Sub-editors, in particular, must know what it is they are doing – otherwise their intervention in copy is inconsistent, arbitrary and pointless.

Certainly, when you know the rules of grammar, you can, where appropriate, break them: write 'who' for 'whom' in the sentence 'Whom did you invite?'; 'It's me' instead of 'It is I'; 'painters like Picasso' instead of 'painters such as Picasso'. At least then you will know what you are doing and be able to defend it.

But there is never an excuse for sentences like this one:

> After all, my responses were no different to those employers who reject candidates on grounds that would make me fume if I read about them in a newspaper.
>
> (*Guardian*, 19 January 1993)

What the writer means is something completely different: replace 'no different to those employers' by 'no different from those of employers' and the meaning becomes clear. Follow the rules of grammar (different *from*; always compare like with like) and you will avoid this sort of mistake.

This book is less prescriptive than some others on the question of vocabulary. It takes as a premise that words mean what people in general, rather than academics in particular, say they mean. Thus, if most people now use 'celibate' to mean 'abstaining from sex' rather than 'unmarried', or 'regularly' to mean 'often' rather than 'at regular intervals', it is pointless to say that they are wrong. And it is foolish to follow the dictionary where the dictionary conflicts with usage.

The best advice with such words is to use them with care; if in doubt, find an alternative. Here, as everywhere, your guiding principle must be: what will my reader understand by the words I use?

CHAPTER 2

GRAMMAR: THE RULES

Grammar is the set of rules and conventions that are the basis of the language.

Early English grammars were derived from the rules of Latin. The result was that they were over-rigid and even included 'rules' that did not apply to English at all. For example, there is no rule of English grammar that prohibits split infinitives, or prepositions to end sentences, or conjunctions to start them. These are matters of style not grammar.

In the 1960s English grammar was accused of restricting the personal development and free expression of young people. The previously accepted form of standard English was declared to be both a straitjacket on self-expression and a devious means of keeping the working class and ethnic minorities in their place. The result was that in many politically correct classrooms the teaching of English grammar was virtually abandoned.

But the pendulum has swung back, and learning the rules of grammar is now an important part of the national curriculum. This is surely right – above all, for journalists, who act as interpreters between the sources they use and their readers and listeners. Not to know the grammar of their own language is a big disadvantage for a writer – and a crippling one for a sub-editor.

A comprehensive English grammar would constitute a book of its own. What follows is an attempt to list the main grammatical terms and rules you need to know. The next chapter describes common mistakes and confusions.

Note: the term 'syntax', meaning grammatical structure in sentences, is not used in this book. Instead the general term 'grammar' is used to cover both the parts of speech and the structure of sentences.

THE PARTS OF SPEECH

There are eight parts of speech: noun, pronoun, adjective, verb, adverb, preposition, conjunction and interjection.

NOUN

Nouns are the names of people and things. They are either ordinary nouns called *common* ('thing', 'chair') or special nouns called *proper* ('George', 'Tuesday'). Proper nouns generally take a capital letter.

Abstract common nouns refer to qualities ('beauty', 'honesty'), emotions ('anger', 'pity') or states ('friendship', 'childhood').

In general nouns are *singular* ('thing', 'man') or *plural* ('things', 'men'). But some nouns are the same in the singular and the plural ('aircraft', 'sheep') and some are used only in the plural ('scissors', 'trousers'). Nouns that refer to collections of people and things ('the cabinet', 'the team') are known as *collective* nouns.

PRONOUN

Pronouns stand for nouns and are often used to avoid repetition. They can be:

personal ('I', 'yours', 'him')
reflexive/intensive ('myself', 'herself', 'themselves')
relative/interrogative ('who', 'whose', 'whom')
indefinite ('anybody', 'none', 'each').

The noun that a pronoun stands for is called its *antecedent*.

Pronouns, unlike nouns, often change their form according to the role they play in a sentence: 'I' becomes 'me'; 'you' becomes 'yours'. This role of a noun or pronoun is called *case*. Following the Latin model, grammarians used to talk about such things as the nominative, dative and genitive cases. But this is needlessly complicated: the key distinction is between the *subjective* case ('I') and the *objective* case ('me').

VERB

Verbs express action or a state of being. They are called *finite* because they have a subject ('He thinks') or *non-finite* because they do not ('to think').

Finite verbs

Mood: verbs are either

indicative, that is statement or question ('He sees the ball'/'Does he see the ball?')

imperative ('Go on, hit the ball')
subjunctive ('If he were to see the ball . . .').

Indicative tenses

There are three basic times (present, past, future) and three basic actions (simple, completed, continuing). Thus there are nine basic tenses:

	Simple	*Continuing*	*Completed*
Present	I see	I am seeing	I have seen
Past	I saw	I was seeing	I had seen
Future	I shall see	I shall be seeing	I shall have seen

Three other tenses show a mixture of continuing and completed action:

Present: I have been seeing
Past: I had been seeing
Future: I shall have been seeing

Grammarians traditionally distinguish between the first person singular ('I'), the second person singular ('thou'), the third person singular ('he/she'), the first person plural ('we'), the second person plural ('you') and the third person plural ('they'). But modern English has dispensed with the second person singular ('thou' is archaic), and in most verbs only the third person singular differs from the standard form:

I see
He/she sees
We see
You see
They see

Subjunctive tenses

The verb forms for the subjunctive mood are much the same as for the indicative. But there are two exceptions.

The third person singular, present tense, changes as follows:

'She *has* faith' becomes 'If she *have* faith'
'He *finds*' becomes 'Should he *find*'.

The verb 'to be' changes as follows:

	Present
Indicative	*Subjunctive*
	(if)
I am	I be
He/she is	He/she be

We are	We be
You are	You be
They are	They be

	Past
Indicative	*Subjunctive*
	(if)
I was	I were
He/she was	He/she were

'We were', 'you were' and 'they were' remain unchanged.

Non-finite verbs

There are three types of non-finite verb:

1 the *infinitive* ('to see')
2 the *present participle* ('seeing')
3 the *past participle* ('seen').

Note that 'to' is sometimes omitted from the infinitive. 'I want *to see*' and 'I can't *see*' are both examples of the infinitive.

The participles are used to make up the basic tenses (see above).

The present participle is also used as a noun ('seeing is believing'), as an adjective ('a far-seeing statesman') and in phrases (see *Phrases*, pp12–13).

The past participle is also used as an adjective ('an unseen passage') and in phrases.

ADJECTIVE

An adjective describes a noun or pronoun.

The most common adjectives are the *definite article* (the) and the *indefinite article* (a, an).

Demonstrative adjectives (this, that, these, those) identify a noun ('this car', 'these potatoes'). When used without a noun they become pronouns ('This is my car').

Possessive adjectives (my, your, our) show ownership ('my car').

Most other adjectives are *absolute adjectives* (final, perfect) or *adjectives of degree*.

Adjectives of degree are either

positive, used of a thing ('hot', 'complicated')

comparative, used to compare one thing with another ('hotter', 'more complicated')

superlative, used to compare a thing with two or more others ('hottest', 'most complicated').

ADVERB

An adverb usually describes a verb, adjective or other adverb:

He sees *clearly* [adverb describes verb].
It was a *newly* minted coin [adverb describes adjective].
He sees *very* clearly [adverb describes adverb].

Some adverbs are used to link sentences; they are called *sentence adverbs* or *conjunctive adverbs* and are usually marked off by commas:

Life is expensive. Death, *however*, is cheap.

Note that 'however' can also be used as an ordinary adverb:

However good you may be at punctuation, you will still make mistakes.

PREPOSITION

A preposition is a word that links its object with a preceding word or phrase:

It's a case *of* mumps.
We're going *to* Blackpool.

When the object of a preposition is a pronoun it must be in the objective case. Thus:

of me
to her
for him
by us
with them

CONJUNCTION

A conjunction is a word that:

1 links two similar parts of speech

fit *and* well
slowly *but* surely

2 links two sentences whether or not they are separated by a full stop

You may come. *Or* you may go.
You may come *or* you may go.

3 links main clauses with subordinate clauses and phrases

I will *if* you will.
I will go *as* a clown.

INTERJECTION

An interjection is a short exclamation that is outside the main sentence. It either stands alone or is linked to the sentence by a comma:

Alas! Woe is me!
Hello, how are you?

SENTENCES

A sentence is a group of words expressing a complete thought. It must have a *subject*, the person or thing being discussed, and it must have a *verb*, expressing action or a state of being:

Subject	*verb*
The man	sees.

The subject may be understood rather than stated:

The old man lay down. And died.

In the second sentence 'he' is understood.

TRANSITIVE VERBS AND OBJECTS

A sentence may have an *object*, the person or thing that receives the action of the verb. This kind of verb is called *transitive*:

Subject	*verb*	*object*
The man	sees	the sun.

An object may be *direct* or *indirect*:

Subject	*verb*	*direct object*	*indirect object*
The man	gives	the dog	to his son.

Subject	verb	indirect object	direct object
The man	gives	the dog	a bone.

Note that 'to' is sometimes, but not always, included with an indirect object.

INTRANSITIVE VERBS

If nothing receives the action of the verb it is *intransitive*:

Subject	verb
The man	walks.

If an intransitive verb is followed by something to extend or complete its meaning this is not called an object:

The man walks slowly [adverb].
The man walks to work [adverbial phrase].

ACTIVE AND PASSIVE VERBS

A transitive verb is in the *active voice*. It can also be turned round so that it is in the *passive voice*:

Active
The man sees the sun.
Passive
The sun is seen by the man.

Be careful when you combine the passive with a participle:

The workers were penalised by sending them back.

is incorrect because the subject of both main verb and participle must be the same. Instead write either:

They penalised the workers by sending them back.

or:

The workers were penalised by being sent back.

INACTIVE VERBS AND COMPLEMENTS

If a verb expresses not action but a state of being it is inactive and takes a *complement*.

Subject	*verb*	*complement*
The man	is	ill.
He	feels	a fool.

Note that some verbs can be either transitive or inactive:

He feels ill [complement].
He feels the cloth [object].

Note that both direct and indirect objects are in the objective case but that complements, like their subjects, are in the subjective case:

I see him [object].
I am he [complement].

AGREEMENT OF THE VERB

The verb must agree with its subject in person and number:

I give.

but:

He gives [person].

Spelling is important.

but:

Spelling and grammar are important [number].

1   Note that words joined to a single subject by a preposition do not affect the verb:

Spelling, with grammar, is important.

2   If two subjects are linked by 'either, or' or 'neither, nor' the verb agrees with the nearer subject:

Neither the news editor nor any of his reporters have received the call.

3   If one subject is affirmative and the other negative the verb agrees with the affirmative one:

The chief sub, not her deputies, was at lunch.

4   Nouns that are plural in form but singular in meaning take a singular verb:

News is what the reader wants to know.
Thirty pages is a lot of copy.

5   The word 'number' is treated as singular when it is a figure but as plural when it means 'a few':

A number is stamped on each computer.

but:

A number of computers are needed.

6   Singular pronouns such as 'everyone' take a singular verb. 'None' can be either singular or plural:

Are there any bananas? No, there are none.
Is there any beer? No, there is none.

7   Collective nouns take either a singular or a plural verb according to sense:

The team is small [it has few players].

but:

The team are small [its players are not big].

The cabinet is determined [it is seen as a single body].

but:

The cabinet are discussing [it takes at least two to discuss].

The cabinet is divided [it must be seen as one before it can be divided].

but:

The cabinet are agreed [it takes more than one to agree].

Do not mix the two forms. Do not write:

The cabinet is divided but they are discussing . . .

Note that many house-style books insist on organisations being treated as singular. If this is your style, follow it.

SENTENCE STRUCTURE

A sentence with only one verb is a *simple* sentence:

The man sees the sun.

A sentence with two or more main verbs is a *compound* sentence:

The man sees the sun and he closes his eyes.

A sentence with one or more main verbs and one or more subsidiary verbs is a *complex* sentence:

The man who sees the sun closes his eyes.

CLAUSES

A clause is a group of words including a subject and a verb forming part of a sentence. A compound sentence has two or more main clauses; a complex sentence has at least one main clause and at least one subordinate clause. In the sentence above the main clause is 'The man closes his eyes' and the subordinate clause is 'who sees the sun'.

A distinction must be made between clauses that define and those that do not. Consider the sentence above with and without commas:

The man who sees the sun closes his eyes [in general a man who sees the sun will close his eyes].
The man, who sees the sun, closes his eyes [this particular man, having seen the sun, closes his eyes].

With things the distinction can be made clear by using 'that' to define and 'which' in a non-restrictive way:

This is the house that Jack built [clause defines the house].
Fred's house, which was built in 1937, is up for sale [clause does not restrict, adds incidental information].

With people, too, 'that' can be used to define:

This is the man that I told you about.

But 'which' cannot be used of people.
So where the clause defines, use 'that' (or 'who' of people) and do not use commas; where the clause does not define, use 'which' (or 'who' of people) and include commas.

A final test is: can you omit the subordinate clause altogether without making the main clause meaningless? If you can, always use 'which' (or 'who') of people and include commas.

PHRASES

A phrase is a group of words without a verb forming part of a sentence.
An adjectival phrase must be related to the correct noun or pronoun.

A readable book, it has a good index.
Correct: the phrase 'a readable book' describes the subject 'it'.

A readable book, its value is enhanced by a good index.
Incorrect: the phrase 'a readable book' cannot describe the subject 'its value'.

Like Belfast, Beirut has known civil war.
Correct: the phrase 'like Belfast' describes the subject 'Beirut'.

Unlike Belfast, bomb blasts no longer echo across the city.
Incorrect: the phrase 'unlike Belfast' cannot describe the subject 'bomb blasts'.

This mistake is called the dangling modifier. A particularly common example of it is the dangling, floating or hanging participle:

Walking across the road, he was run over by a car.
Correct: the phrase 'walking across the road' describes the subject 'he'.

Walking across the road, a car ran him over.
Incorrect: the phrase 'walking across the road' cannot describe the subject 'a car'.

CHAPTER 3

GRAMMAR: MISTAKES AND CONFUSIONS

A AND AN

Words with a silent 'h' such as 'honest' take 'an' instead of 'a':

an honest man

Unless your style book directs, do not extend this to such words as 'hotel' and 'historian'.

ABSOLUTE ADJECTIVES

Do not misuse absolute adjectives such as

absolute	ideal
basic	impossible
complete	obvious
empty	perfect
essential	pure
fatal	ultimate
final	unique
full	

A thing is either perfect or less than perfect. It cannot be 'more perfect' or 'most perfect'. It is similarly ludicrous to write 'more fatal' or 'more unique'.

AND AND BUT

See *Conjunctions to start sentences*, p16.

AND WHICH

Do not write 'and which' unless it follows 'which'. For example, do not write:

The incomes policy, announced last week by the government *and which* aims to control inflation, is supported by the opposition.

AS GOOD AS

If 'as good as' is followed by 'if not better than', do not omit the second 'as':

He is as good, if not better, than I am.

Either write:

He is as good as, if not better than, I am.

or, better:

He is as good as I am, if not better.

BETWEEN AND AMONG

Use 'between' of two people or things; 'among' of three or more people or things. But also use 'between' to show a relationship between one person/thing and several others:

There is no love lost between my brothers and me.

BETWEEN/AND

'Between' must be followed by 'and'. Do not write 'between 1914–18'. Write either 'in 1914–18' or 'between 1914 and 1918'.

BOTH

Do not use 'both' when it is unnecessary:

John and Mary were both talking to each other.

CENTRE ON, IN AND AROUND

See *Prepositions: the pitfalls*, pp20–1.

COMPARE LIKE WITH LIKE

Be careful to compare like with like. Do not write:

Fred's efforts were better than Jim.
France's exports were worth more than Italy.

COMPARE TO AND WITH

Use 'with' for routine comparisons – like with like, last year's figures with this year's. Use 'to' when the comparison itself makes a point as in:

Shall I compare thee to a summer's day?

COMPRISE (OF)

See *Prepositions: the pitfalls*, pp20–1.

CONJUNCTIONS TO START SENTENCES

The Bible, Shakespeare and Keith Waterhouse all sanction the use of 'and' and 'but' to start sentences. And whatever your English teacher may have said to the contrary, this practice is not a grammatical mistake.

Nor is it a grammatical mistake to write:

Because the food was awful they walked out.

But subordinate clauses starting with conjunctions such as 'because', 'while' and 'though' should not be used as stand-alone sentences as in:

They walked out. Because the food was awful.
They walked out. Though they had paid for the meal in advance.

The point is that here – and almost everywhere – the reader expects a sentence starting with 'because', 'while' or 'though' to have a main clause.

You can sometimes get away with the device by preparing the reader for it:

Why did they walk out? Because the food was awful.

But don't overdo it.

DANGLING MODIFIERS

See Chapter 2, *Grammar* p13.

DIFFERENT FROM, TO AND THAN

See *Prepositions: the pitfalls*, pp20–1.

DUE TO

'Due' is an adjective and is also used in adjectival phrases:

The rent is *due*.
The cancellation is *due to bad weather*.

Strict grammarians – and many house-style books – say that 'due to' may not be used to introduce an adverbial phrase; that what follows is a mistake:

The train was cancelled *due to bad weather*.

So the best advice, whatever British Rail may say, is: don't do it.

EQUALLY

Do not write 'equally as good': 'equally' means 'as . . . as'. Either write:

He is as good as gold.

or:

He is equally good.

FEWER AND LESS

Distinguish between 'fewer', which refers to number, and 'less', which refers to volume:

Fewer strawberries in the fields results in *less* fruit in the shops.
If there are *fewer* trees there will be *less* wood.

Above all, do not write 'less' of people as in:

Less people know grammar nowadays.

FLOATING, HANGING PARTICIPLES

See Chapter 2, *Grammar*, p13.

FOR YOU AND I

Avoid being posh – and wrong at the same time. The preposition 'for', like all the rest, must be followed by the objective case: always write 'for me' not 'for I'.

FROM/TO

'From' must be followed by 'to'. Do not write 'from 1939–45'. Write either 'in 1939–45' or 'from 1939 to 1945'.

HOPEFULLY

Expressions such as 'hopefully' and 'generally speaking', although they are, strictly speaking, 'dangling modifiers' (see Chapter 2, *Grammar*, p13), are increasingly accepted in everyday journalism.

But avoid imprecision. In 'Generally speaking, grammar is important' and 'Hopefully, your punctuation will improve' the speaker/writer expresses an opinion, but it is not clear who shares it. Where it is important to be precise, always write:

I hope your punctuation will improve.

or:

Let *us* hope your punctuation will improve.

LAY AND LIE

Do not confuse 'lay' and 'lie' as many Americans do, particularly in pop songs. 'Lay' is a transitive verb and so takes an object; 'lie' is an intransitive verb and does not:

Chickens *lay* eggs.
Waiters *lay* the table.
Soldiers *lay down* their arms.

but:

A sun-worshipper *lies down* on the beach.

LIKE AND SUCH AS

Do not confuse 'like' and 'such as'. 'Like' makes a comparison; 'such as' introduces examples:

Fruit trees, like flowers, need water.
Fruit trees such as the plum and the cherry need pruning.

If you write 'Fruit trees like the plum and the cherry . . .' you imply that the plum and cherry are not fruit trees.

MAY AND MIGHT

Do not confuse 'may' and 'might': they are different tenses of the same verb.

'First aid may have saved him' suggests that he had first aid and we do not yet know whether he will survive.

'First aid might have saved him' suggests that he did not have first aid but if he had, it is possible that he would have survived.

MEET

Do not use 'with' (still less 'up with') when 'meet' means 'come face to face with' (a person):

Fred met Joan at the station.

Use 'with' when 'meet' means 'chance to experience' as in:

He met with an accident.

ONE AND YOU

Do not mix the two impersonal pronouns 'one' and 'you'. Either write:

If one wants to be a journalist, one should learn to use one's eyes.

or, better:

If you want to be a journalist, you should learn to use your eyes.

Do not write:

If one wants to be a journalist, you should learn to use your eyes.

In general use 'you': leave the formal 'one' to the royal family.

ONLY

Be careful with 'only': putting this word in the wrong place can affect the meaning of a sentence.

'I'm only here for the beer' is unlikely to be misunderstood, but what is meant by 'He only eats here on Tuesdays'? That on Tuesdays he refrains from drinking? Or that he eats here only on Tuesdays?

To be clear, put 'only' directly before the word or phrase it refers to.

PREPOSITIONS TO END SENTENCES

Ending a sentence with a preposition may sometimes be bad style but it is not bad grammar. As Winston Churchill once wrote (defending his own writing from redrafting by a pedantic civil servant): 'This is something up with which I will not put.'

So, where your ear tells you that a preposition can go at the end of the sentence, put it there.

PREPOSITIONS: THE PITFALLS

The most common mistake is to use the wrong preposition or to use one where it is not necessary. Note the following examples of commonly misused prepositions:

acquiesce *in* (not *to*)
affinity *between* (not *to*)
agree *on* (a point), *to* (a proposal), *with* (a person or opinion)
alien *from* (not *to*)
arise *from* (not *out of*)
bored *with* (not *of*)
compare: see p16
centre *on/in* (not *around*)
comprise: no preposition (do not use *of*)
consider: no preposition (do not use *as*)
correspond *with* (a person), *to* (a thing)
die *of* (not *from*)
differ *from* (in comparisons, not *to* or *than*), *with* (a person when disagreeing)
different *from* (not *to* or *than*)
dissent *from* (not *to*)
fed up *with* (not *of*)

glad *at* (a piece of news), *of* (a possession)
impatient *for* (a thing), *with* (a person)
independent *of* (not *from*)
martyr *for* (a cause), *to* (a disease)
meet: see p19
oblivious *of* (not *from*)
part *from* (a person), *with* (a thing)
prevail *against* (a thing), *on* (a person)
protest *at/against*
reconcile *to* (a thing), *with* (a person)
taste *of* (food), *for* (the arts and other things).

Most compound prepositions are an abomination. Avoid such expressions as:

in connection with
in regard to
in relation to.

SPLIT INFINITIVE

'To boldly go' is a split infinitive: the infinitive is divided by an adverb. It is often bad style but it is not bad grammar.

In deciding whether or not to split the infinitive ask yourself:

1 Is the adverb superfluous? Often it contributes nothing to the sense.
2 Would the adverb be better somewhere else in the sentence?
3 Would the sentence sound better/make better sense if it were rewritten?

If the answer to these questions is no, split away.

SUPERLATIVES

Do not use the superlative where you should use the comparative. For example, you cannot have 'the least of two evils' or 'the best of two games' or 'the eldest of two brothers'. And do not use a double superlative such as 'most fondest'.

THAT AND WHICH

See Chapter 2, *Grammar*, p12.

TRY TO/AND

After 'try' use the infinitive form not a conjunction. Write 'try *to* write' not 'try *and* write'.

WHO AND WHOM

Most people say and write '*Who* did you invite to dinner?' although the correct form is '*Whom* did you invite?'

In tabloids and popular magazines the informal, 'incorrect' form is acceptable.

Some journalists who wish to be formal write:

Whom did you say came to dinner?

This is a mistake, since 'whom' here is the subject of the sentence: it should be '*Who* did you say came to dinner?'

CHAPTER 4

SPELLING

English spelling often defies logic. Why should we spell 'harass' with one 'r' and 'embarrass' with two? Why does 'mantelpiece' echo its Latin origin (*mantellum*, cloak) while 'mantle', the posh word for 'cloak', does not? Why does 'dependent' (the adjective) differ from 'dependant' (the noun)?

Whereas punctuation evolves, spelling does not. Whereas with grammar and punctuation you can sometimes argue a case for loose, colloquial usage, with spelling there is no way out. The word is either right or wrong – though some words are spelt in more than one way (see Chapter 7, *House style*, pp48–50).

Nobody expects you to know how to spell all the words in the dictionary. The key thing is to avoid mistakes: learn to recognise the words you cannot spell and look them up.

WORDS PEOPLE GET WRONG

First, here's a list of words that many people can't spell. Get somebody to test you on it.

abhorrence	clamouring
accidentally	connoisseur
accommodation	consensus
acquiescence	convertible
annihilate	corpuscle
asphyxiate	corroborate
authoritative	
auxiliary	debatable
	definitely
benefited	descendant
blamable	desiccated
bureaucracy	destructible
	diagrammatic
Caribbean	diarrhoea

dignitary
dispel
dissatisfaction
dysentery

ecstasy
effervescence
eligibility
embarrass
emissary
exaggerate
exhilaration
expatriate

fallacious
forty
fulfilling
funereal

gaseous

haemorrhage
harass
heinous
herbaceous
hiccup
humorous
hygiene
hysterical

idiosyncrasy
indissoluble
innocuous
innuendo
inoculate
intestacy
iridescence

jeopardise

kitchenette

liaison
licentious

linchpin
loquacious

maintenance
manoeuvre
mantelpiece
meanness
Mediterranean
millennium
miniature
minuscule
miscellaneous
mischievous

negotiate
nonchalant
noticeable

obeisance
occurred
omitted
oscillate

paraphernalia
perspicacious
plummeted
predilection
privilege
profession
proprietary
pseudonym
publicly
pursue

recommend
reconnaissance
referred
restaurateur
resuscitate
riveted

separate
statutory
supersede

targeted   unparalleled
tranquillity

                        vacillate
unforeseen   veterinary
unnecessary   vociferous

CONFUSIONS

(*See also* Chapter 9, *Words* pp67–9.)

One reason why people misspell some words is that they confuse them with other words. There are three common kinds of confusion:

1 a word is confused with a shorter one that sounds the same

consensus	(census)
supersede	(cede)
minuscule	(mini)
dispel	(spell)
fulfil	(full/fill)
playwright	(write)
skilful	(skill/full)

2 a word is confused with a different one that sounds the same

aural	oral
born	borne
breach	breech
cannon	canon
complement	compliment
cord	chord
counsel	council
curb	kerb
draft	draught
discreet	discrete
expatriate	ex-patriot
forbear	forebear
forego	forgo
foreword	forward
grisly	grizzly
hanger	hangar
horde	hoard
lead (the metal)	led (the past participle)
lightening	lightning

metal	mettle
principal	principle
review	revue
sight	site
stationary	stationery
storey	story
swat	swot
toe	tow
way	weigh.

3 a word used as one part of speech is confused with the same word used as another part of speech

Noun	*Verb*
practice	practise, *so also* practising, practised
licence	license, *so also* licensing, licensed
envelope	envelop, *so also* enveloping, enveloped.

Noun	*Adjective*
dependant	dependent.

In one of the pairs listed above the words are pronounced differently:

Noun	*Verb*
*en*velope	en*vel*op.

If you find it difficult to distinguish between the common pairs *practic(s)e* and *licenc(s)e*, note that *advic(s)e* changes its pronunciation as well as spelling and remember the three pairs together:

Noun	*Verb*
advice	advise
practice	practise
licence	license

or remember the sentence:

Doctors need a licence to practise.

In this case the noun ('c') comes before the verb ('s').

I BEFORE E

Most people know the spelling rule 'i' before 'e' except after 'c'. This gives:

believe, niece, siege

and:

ceiling, deceive, receive.

But note that the rule applies only to the 'ee' sound and that there are exceptions such as:

caffeine, codeine, counterfeit, protein, seize

and, in the other direction:

species.

PLURALS

1 Nouns ending in a consonant followed by 'y' take 'ies' in the plural:

lady	*ladies*
penny	*pennies*
story	*stories.*

But proper nouns take the standard 's' in the plural:

the two Germanys
three Hail Marys
four Pennys in a class list.

And nouns ending in a vowel followed by 'y' take the standard 's' in the plural:

donkey	*donkeys*
monkey	*monkeys*
storey	*storeys.*

2 Most nouns ending in 'o' take the standard 's' but some common ones take 'es' in the plural:

buffaloes, cargoes, dingoes, dominoes, echoes, embargoes, goes, heroes, mangoes, mottoes, negroes, noes, potatoes, tomatoes, tornadoes, torpedoes, vetoes, volcanoes.

And some may be spelt either with 's' or 'es':

archipelago, banjo, grotto, halo, innuendo, memento, mosquito, salvo.

3 Some nouns that come from Greek, Latin or modern languages keep their original plural form:

addendum	*addenda*
alumna	*alumnae*
alumnus	*alumni*
bacillus	*bacilli*
chateau	*chateaux*
criterion	*criteria*

minimum   *minima*
phenomenon   *phenomena*
spectrum   *spectra.*

In some cases both the original plural form and an anglicised version are used:

appendix	*appendices* (used of books)	*appendixes* (used of both books and the body)
beau	*beaux*	*beaus*
bureau	*bureaux*	*bureaus*
cactus	*cacti*	*cactuses*
formula	*formulae* (scientific)	*formulas* (general use)
fungus	*fungi*	*funguses*
index	*indices* (mathematics)	*indexes* (books)
medium	*media* (the press, etc.)	*mediums* (spiritualism)
memorandum	*memoranda*	*memorandums*
plateau	*plateaux*	*plateaus*
syllabus	*syllabi*	*syllabuses*
terminus	*termini*	*terminuses*
virtuoso	*virtuosi*	*virtuosos.*

Be careful of confusing the singular with the plural when the latter form is more common as with:

graffito   *graffiti*
die   *dice*
stratum   *strata.*

But note that plurals such as 'agenda', 'data' and 'media' are often treated as though they were singular. Check your house style.

SUFFIXES

1 One-syllable words with a short vowel and a single final consonant double it before a suffix that starts with a vowel.

fat   *fatten, fatter*
run   *runner, running.*

2 So, too, do words with more than one syllable if the stress is on the final syllable.

begin   *beginning, beginner*
refer   *referred, referral*
prefer   *preferred* – but note *prefer*able (pronounced *prefer*able).

3 But one-syllable words with a long vowel or double vowel do not double the final consonant.

seat   *seated, seating*
look   *looking, looked.*

4 Nor do words with more than one syllable if the stress is before the final syllable.

proffer   *proffer, proffering*
benefit   *benefiting, benefited*
leaflet   *leafleting, leafleter.*

5 Exceptions to these rules include most words ending in 'l':

cavil   *cavilling*
devil   *devilled* (but *devilish*)
level   *levelled*
revel   *reveller*
travel   *traveller*
but:
parallel   *paralleled*

and some words ending in 'p' or 's':

worship   *worshipped*
bus   *buses*
gas   *gases*

while some words ending in 's' are optional:

bias   *biased* or *biassed*
focus   *focused* or *focussed.*

House style determines whether the extra 's' is added.

6 Sometimes the stress changes when a noun is used as a verb:

format   *formative* but *formatted* (in computer speak).

Dictionaries generally give:

combat   combatant   combative   combated.

But there is an argument for 'combatted' on the grounds that some people pronounce it that way. (You can, of course, avoid the problem altogether by using 'fight' as a verb instead of 'combat': it's one character shorter.)

7 Words ending in a silent 'e' keep it if the suffix begins with a consonant:

safe   safety
same   sameness.

But note that there are common exceptions:

due   duty
true   truly
awe   awful (but awesome)
wide   width.

And some words are optional:

acknowledg(e)ment, judg(e)ment.

8 Words ending in a silent 'e' drop it if the suffix begins with a vowel:

bake   baking
sane   sanity

but:

change changeable
mile   mileage.

Note that 'y' here acts as a vowel:

gore   gory
ice   icy.

9 Sometimes keeping or losing the silent 'e' makes it possible to distinguish
two words with different meanings:

dying (the death)   dyeing (clothes)
linage (payment by the line)   lineage (descent)
singing (musically)   singeing (burning)
swinging (from a tree)   swingeing (heavy).

AGREEMENT

A few French words have an extra 'e' for the feminine form:

blond(e), confidant(e), divorcée.

Note that in French an adjective agrees with its noun not the person the
adjective refers to. Thus (since hair has no gender in English):

A blonde woman has blond hair.

This logical point is made in several house-style books – but generally ignored.

'Chaperon(e)' is a curiosity. In French '*chaperon*' exists only as a masculine noun; in English the (false) feminine form 'chaperone' is far more common.

CHAPTER 5

PUNCTUATION

The point of punctuation is to make reading easy. It is the written counter-part of the pauses and inflections that make speech understandable. But be careful: it does not necessarily follow that everywhere you would pause in speech you punctuate in writing. And sometimes the strength of a punctuation mark differs from the length of the equivalent pause in speech.

Ideally, punctuation should be based on sound logical principles. But be careful: do not try to force your punctuation practice into a format that defies current usage.

One modern school of thought says: the less punctuation the better. And it is certainly true that there is less punctuation than there used to be, for all sorts of reasons: sentences are shorter so they need fewer intermediate stops; as abbreviations become familiar they no longer need to be marked as such; designers dislike dots . . . But be careful: don't be ultra-modern or you risk confusing your reader.

THE FOUR MAIN STOPS

These are: the comma, the semicolon, the colon and the full stop. Of these the comma is the weakest and the full stop the strongest with the colon and semicolon somewhere in between. Some books still say that the colon is a stronger stop than the semicolon – and it can be – but it isn't always stronger. It makes more sense to say that the semicolon lies midway between a comma and a full stop while the colon now has a series of specialist uses.

THE COMMA

1 Use the comma to separate a series of words of the same kind:

The reporter should always write clear, concise, accurate English.

but do not use the comma when a series of adjectives is cumulative:

He ordered a rich chocolate sponge cake.

Note that there is usually no comma before the 'and' at the end of a list of single words:

She said the same to James, Stephen, Mark and John.

2 Use the comma to separate a series of phrases of the same kind:

His writing was more refined, more intellectual, more Latinate, than Smith's.

Use a comma before the 'and' at the end of a list where it helps to prevent confusion:

They invited Charles and Mary, Andrew and Susan, and Anne.

3 Use the comma to mark off words that address somebody or something:

Come on, City.

4 Use the comma, where appropriate, to mark off words or phrases such as 'however', 'for example', 'in fact', 'of course':

With punctuation, however, it pays to be careful.

Note that many journalists now omit the comma in most such cases – but you should always include it if there is any chance of misunderstanding.

5 Use the comma to mark off a word in parenthesis:

Born in Little Rock, Arkansas, he went to Washington.

6 Use the comma to mark off a phrase in parenthesis:

Norman Mailer's first novel, The Naked and the Dead, was a bestseller.

Do not use the comma where the phrase is essential to the meaning of the sentence:

Norman Mailer's novel The Naked and the Dead was a bestseller.

Note that in this example commas would mean that Mailer had written only one novel.

Also note the difference between '*the Home Secretary, Michael Howard,*' and '*Michael Howard, the Home Secretary,*' (both parenthetical, so commas) and '*Home Secretary Michael Howard*' and '*the Tory MP Michael Howard*' (not parenthetical, so no commas).

7 Use the comma to mark off a clause in parenthesis:

The paper's subs, who were in their shirt sleeves, worked fast.

Do not use the comma where the clause is essential to the meaning of the sentence:

The subs who were in their shirt sleeves worked fast; those who were wearing summer dresses worked even faster.

But note the example below which breaks this rule:

Those who can, do; those who can't, teach.

8 Use the comma, where necessary, to mark off an introductory phrase or clause:

Because of the appalling weather, conditions for holidaymakers were described as 'intolerable'.

Where a phrase or clause that needs commas follows a conjunction such as 'but' or 'and', the first comma is now considered to be optional:

Fred tried to get up but (,) because he was tired and emotional, he failed.

9 Use the comma, where two sentences are joined by a conjunction, if you want to lengthen the pause:

He wanted to leave the party, but his friend detained him.

Do not use the comma where the subject of the two sentences is the same:

He wanted to leave but didn't.

Do not use the comma between sentences where there is no conjunction: Avoid:

He wanted to leave, his friend detained him.

But note the example below of a series of short sentences where the comma can be used:

I came, I saw, I conquered.

THE SEMICOLON

1 Use the semicolon between sentences, with or without a conjunction, as a longer pause than a comma and a shorter one than a full stop:

The rumour was that the king was dead; the people believed it.
There will be an inquest, of course; but the matter will not end there.

2 Use the semicolon to separate longer items in a list, particularly if the items themselves need further punctuation by commas:

Punctuation marks include the full stop, which is the strongest stop; the semicolon, which is weaker; and the comma, which is weakest of all.

THE COLON

1 Use the colon, in preference to the comma, to introduce full-sentence quotes:

He said: 'Punctuation is difficult.'

2 Use the colon to introduce lists:

All of them were dead: Bill, Jack, Ted and Willie.

3 Use the colon between two sentences where the second explains or justifies the first:

Keep your language uncluttered: it reads more easily.

4 Use the colon between two sentences to mark an antithesis:

Man proposes: God disposes.

5 Use the colon in a caption to connect the person or object in the picture with the rest of the caption:

Napoleon: 'Victory is ours'
Victorious: Napoleon

THE FULL STOP (FULL POINT, PERIOD)

Use the full stop in text to mark the end of a sentence. You do not need to use full stops after headlines, standfirsts, captions and other forms of displayed type: remember that white space punctuates. See Chapter 7, *House style*, pp48–50, on the use of full stops after initials and abbreviations.

QUOTATION MARKS (QUOTE MARKS, QUOTES)

1 Use quote marks for direct speech: see Chapter 6, *Reporting speech*, pp43–7.

2 Use quote marks for extracts from written reports, following the same rules as for speech.

3 Use quote marks in a headline to show that an assertion is made by

somebody in the story rather than by your publication: this can be vital in court stories.

4 Whether you use double or single quotes in text is a matter of house style, but in headlines always use single quotes.

5 For quotes within quotes use double inside single, and vice versa:

> *He said: 'I really meant to say, "I'm sorry." '*
> *He said: "I really meant to say, 'I'm sorry.' "*

Note that a comma rather than a colon introduces the second quote.

6 Quote marks are sometimes used for the titles of books, plays, etc. – check your house style.

7 Quote marks are sometimes used to emphasise or draw attention to particular words or phrases, to identify slang or technical expressions.

Do not do this unless it is essential for clarity.
Avoid:

> *That double-glazing salesman is a 'cowboy'.*

Either use slang because it fits the context or find another expression.

8 Whether you use single or double quote marks, be consistent. Do not use one form for quoting people and another for book titles and other uses (see Chapter 7, *House style*, pp48–50).

PARENTHESES

1 For a routine, weak parenthesis use commas (see above, pp32–4).

2 To mark a strong but unemphatic parenthesis, usually to explain rather than comment, use round brackets (confusingly they are often called 'parentheses'):

> *the National Union of Mineworkers (NUM)*
> *five miles (about eight kilometres)*
> *Don't call a noisy meeting a shambles (the word means 'slaughterhouse').*

When a parenthesis forms part of a sentence, the full stop comes after the second bracket (as here). (But when the whole sentence is a parenthesis, as here, the full stop comes before the second bracket.)

3 To mark a parenthesis that is added by the writer or editor either to explain or comment, use square brackets:

> *The novelist writes: 'He [the main character] dies in the end.'*
> *'The standard of your spelling and grammer [sic] is terrible.'*

4 To mark a strong, emphatic parenthesis, usually to comment rather than explain, use dashes:

John Smith – the man's a fool – is staying here.

5 The mark that guides the reader to a footnote can be used in journalism.*

OTHER MARKS

THE DASH

1 Use dashes to mark a strong parenthesis (see above).

2 Use the dash, where appropriate, to introduce an explanation or to sum up:

Journalism has many forms – newspaper, periodical, broadcast.

Note that the colon here would do as well – the dash is less formal.

Newspaper, periodical, TV and radio – these are the main forms of journalism.

3 Use the dash to add emphasis or mark a surprise:

This is the point – there's no escaping it.
You'll never guess who wrote the story – Fred Bloggs.

4 Use the dash to mark a change of direction or interruption, particularly in speech:

'I suppose – but what's the use of supposing?'
'I suppose – ' 'Why are you always supposing?'

5 Use either the em (long) dash or the en (short) dash, according to house style.

6 Do not confuse the dash with the hyphen (see below).

THE HYPHEN

1 Use the hyphen for numbers written out:

ninety-nine.

2 Use the hyphen, where appropriate, for compound words such as:

(a) titles:

* But don't overdo it.

vice-president

(b) prefix plus adjective:

extra-marital sex

The sex takes place outside marriage. By contrast 'extra marital sex' suggests married couples working overtime.

(c) adjective plus adjective:

red-hot coals

The first adjective modifies the second.

(d) adverb plus adjective used before the noun:

a well-known fact

But note:

The fact is well known.

Also note that there is no need for a hyphen after adverbs ending in '-ly'. So either write:

a close-knit band of men

or:

a closely knit band of men

(e) adjective plus noun:

a black-cab driver

This refers to the driver of a black (licensed) taxi. By contrast 'black cab driver' may suggest that the driver is black.

(f) noun plus noun:

a black cab-driver

This makes it clear that the driver, rather than the cab, is black.

(g) noun plus preposition plus noun:

mother-in-law

(h) verb plus preposition used as noun:

get-together

But note that when used as a verb, the word does not take the hyphen:

We get together at a get-together.

(i) prefix plus proper noun or adjective:

pre-Christian

(j) prefix plus word to distinguish between meanings:

re-creation (making something again) *recreation* (leisure)

(k) two words that together make a clumsy or ugly juxtaposition:

supra-intestinal
Caithness-shire.

3 Use the hyphen to mark word breaks at the ends of lines.
Note:

(a) with unjustified setting (no right-hand margins) hyphens are less common
(b) avoid a succession of word breaks
(c) when you hyphenate, try to break words into their constituent parts
(d) avoid making unintentional words such as *anal-*
    ysis.

Problem

Double compounds: should it be '*a Jimmy Greaves-type goal*' a '*Jimmy-Greaves-type goal*' or '*a Jimmy Greaves type goal*'?
Solution: Use the first formula unless there is a risk of misunderstanding; then turn the expression round to avoid using the hyphen.

APOSTROPHE

1 Use the apostrophe to show that something is left out of a word:

don't
fo'c's'le

Do not use the apostrophe to show that a word has been shortened.
Avoid:

thro', 'phone, the '60s.

Either use the word in full ('*through*') or in its shortened form without the apostrophe ('*phone*').

2 Use the apostrophe to mark the possessive:

women's liberation, lamb's liver, for goodness' sake

This use is extended to cover 'for' as well as 'of'.

The phrase '*children's books*' means 'books written for children' at least as often as it does 'books owned by children'.

3 Use the apostrophe *where necessary* to make a plural clear:

do's and don'ts

This is easier to read than 'dos and don'ts', although the second is increasingly common.

Mind your p's and q's.

But do not use the apostrophe for routine abbreviations.
Avoid:

Tom's 40p

Instead of the price of tomatoes, it looks like Tom's pocket money.

Common apostrophe mistakes

1 Putting it in where it doesn't belong, for example, *'everything in it's place' 'Apostrophe's are hard to use.'*
2 Leaving it out when it's essential, for example, *'womens liberation'*, *'Its a fact.'*
3 Putting it in the wrong place, for example, *'womens' liberation'*, *'lambs' liver'*.

Apostrophe problems

1 Place names: *King's Langley* but *Kings Norton*.
  Solution: follow usage and use reference books.
2 Names of organisations: *Harrods* but *Christie's*.
  Solution: follow the organisation's own style (check the phone directory) unless it is illiterate: do not write 'womens'.
3 The extra 's': Thomas' or Thomas's?
  Solution: follow sound – if the extra 's' is sounded, as it is in:

St Thomas's

include it; if it is not, as in:

Jesus' disciples

leave it out.

4 The double apostrophe:

Fred's book's title

Solution: avoid it where possible; prefer:

the title of Fred's book.

5 The apostrophe with a title in quotes:

the point of 'Ode to Autumn's' imagery

Solution: avoid – either don't use quotes for titles or write:

the point of the imagery of 'Ode to Autumn'.

THE QUESTION MARK (QUERY)

Use the query after a direct question:

Are you coming?
He asked: 'Are you coming?'

The query is inside the quote marks because the whole question is quoted:

Have you read 'Ode to Autumn'?

The query is outside the quote marks because the question is not part of the quote.

Why is everybody always picking on me?

Although the question may be rhetorical – no answer is expected – it still needs a query.

Common query mistakes

1 Including a query in indirect speech:

He asked if I was coming?

2 Misplacing the query in direct quotes:

He asked: 'Are you coming'?

EXCLAMATION MARK (SCREAMER)

Use the screamer only when it is essential to mark an exclamation:

Ooh, I say!

Do not use the screamer to make comments, signal jokes or mark rhetorical questions.

DOTS (ELLIPSIS, LEADER DOTS)

1 Use three dots to show that something has been omitted, for example from a written quotation. But when you edit quotes in writing up an interview, there is no need to use the dots each time you omit a word.
2 Use three dots to mark a pause:

   I suppose . . . but what's the use of supposing?

3 Use three dots to lead the reader from one headline to another when they are linked:

   Not only . . .
   . . . but also

4 Use dots in charts and tables to make them more readable.

OBLIQUE

Use the oblique to mean either, as in '*and/or*'.

ASTERISK

Use the asterisk (rarely) for footnotes.

CHAPTER 6

REPORTING SPEECH

Reporting speech accurately and clearly is an essential journalistic skill. You must be able to handle both direct quotes and indirectly reported speech.

DIRECT QUOTES

1 When you quote a person for the first time, introduce them before the quote:

> John Smith, the leader of the council, said: 'Of course, I refuse to resign.'

Note that because the quote is a complete sentence, it is introduced by a colon, it starts with a capital letter and the full stop comes before the second quote mark.

2 Subject to house style you can use 'says' instead of 'said':

> John Smith, the leader of the council, says: 'I refuse to resign.'

3 Subject to house style you can use the short form 'council leader':

> Council leader John Smith says: 'I refuse to resign.'

But note:

(a) the style works best when the description is short, say, up to three words: 'company managing director John Smith' is acceptable; 'chairman and managing director John Smith' is probably too long
(b) since the style is supposed to be short and snappy, avoid prepositions such as 'of': 'leader of the council John Smith' is nonsense
(c) since the short description functions as a title, it does not combine well with a real title: 'council leader Dr John Smith' looks and sounds awful and should be avoided.

4 Later in the story variation is possible. Either:

He said: 'I have done nothing wrong.'

or:

'I have done nothing wrong,' he said.

Note that because the quote is a complete sentence, the comma comes before the second quote mark, replacing the full stop in the original.

5 Where the quote is longer than a sentence, put 'he said' either before the quote or after the first complete sentence, not at the end of the quote:

'I'm baffled by the accusations,' he said. 'In fact, I can't see what all the fuss is about.'

6 In features, but not in news, you may break the sentence for effect:

'I'm baffled,' he said, shaking his head, 'by the accusations.'

7 Where a quote continues for more than a paragraph, repeat the quote marks before each new quoted paragraph:

'I'm baffled by the accusations,' he said. 'In fact, I can't see what all the fuss is about.

'I really don't know what to do about the terrible mess I seem to be in.'

Note that there are no closing quote marks after the word 'about'.

8 In general avoid inverting 'Smith' and 'said'. Never write:

Said Smith: 'I will never resign.'

An acceptable use of inversion is where 'Smith' follows the quote and in turn is followed by an explanatory phrase or clause:

'I will never resign,' said Smith, who has been leader of the council for 10 years.

9 You may want to quote a particular word or phrase:

He described himself as 'really baffled'.

Note that here, because the quote is not a complete sentence, the full stop comes after the quote mark.

A word of warning: don't litter your copy with bitty quotes; in general try to quote complete sentences.

10 For quotes within quotes use double quote marks inside single and vice versa:

He said: 'I really meant to say, "I'm sorry." '
He said: "I really meant to say, 'I'm sorry.' "

Note that in both cases a comma rather than a colon introduces the second, enclosed quote.

REPORTED SPEECH

1 The traditional way of reporting speech indirectly is to move most tenses one stage back. Thus the direct quote 'I support electoral reform' becomes:

He said he supported electoral reform.

'I have always supported electoral reform' becomes:

He said he had always supported electoral reform.

'I will always support electoral reform' becomes:

He said he would always support electoral reform.

With the simple past there is usually no change. 'I supported electoral reform until I became leader of the party' becomes:

He said he supported electoral reform until he became leader of the party.
(But it is possible to put 'had' before 'supported' for clarity/emphasis.)

This traditional style has the clear advantage that succeeding paragraphs in the appropriate tense are clearly identified as reported speech:

He said he started supporting electoral reform as a student and did so until he became leader of the party.
Whatever anybody else said, he was still committed to change.

Always follow the correct sequence of tenses: 'is/has' becomes 'was/had'.

2 Journalists increasingly use 'he says' instead of 'he said' for reported speech, even in news stories. Thus 'I support electoral reform' becomes:

He says he supports electoral reform.

'I supported electoral reform until I became leader of the party' becomes:

He says he supported electoral reform until he became leader of the party.

Subject to house style you can use this form – but remember that 'he said' must be used in reporting set-piece events such as speeches, public meetings, courts and tribunals.

3 An advantage of 'he says' over 'he said' is that there is no difficulty in distinguishing between the present 'I support electoral reform' and the past

'I supported electoral reform': the tense remains the same in reported speech. But if you have to use 'he said', it is better to be clear and clumsy than ambiguous. So, where there is the risk of misunderstanding, write:

He said he supports electoral reform.

4 Unless there is a good reason, do not mix your tenses. Do not write 'he said' in one sentence and 'he thinks' in the next.

5 Do not write: 'Speaking at the meeting the speaker said . . .'
Instead write:

The speaker told the meeting . . .

6 Do not follow the fashion of always leaving 'that' out. Leave it out where the subject remains the same:

He says he supports electoral reform.

But include it in most cases where the subject changes:

He says that his opponent supports electoral reform.

Above all, leave 'that' in after words such as 'claims' and 'admits' that have another meaning.
Avoid:

He claims his opponent supports electoral reform.

7 Also, be careful with punctuation. As it stands, the sentence 'John Smith admitted Fred Brown wanted to hit him and did so' could mean several different things:

(a) *John Smith admitted that Fred Brown wanted to hit him and that he did so.*
(b) *John Smith, admitted Fred Brown, wanted to hit him and did so.*
(c) *John Smith admitted [let in] Fred Brown, wanted to hit him – and did so.*

GENERAL POINTS

1 In general, where speakers say things that are nonsensical, obscure or ambiguous, report their words indirectly, telling the reader what they intended to say. For example, do not use 'refute' to mean 'deny' since many people think that to refute an argument is to show that it is false. So if a director says 'I refute your claim that my company is corrupt', write:

The director denied that his company was corrupt.

2 Do not be afraid of repeating 'he says' or 'he said' in your story. The

reader is far more likely to be irritated by awkward variants such as 'commented', 'remarked' and 'stated'. Above all, be careful with 'claimed', 'asserted' (negative) and 'pointed out', 'explained' (positive). Use them only where they are accurate and add weight or colour to the story.

3 Avoid adverbs such as 'wryly' to signal jokes. Do not write:

John Smith describes himself wryly as a plain man in a million.

If the joke is good enough, the reader will not need to be nudged; if it is not, the nudging makes the joke fall flatter.

CHAPTER 7

HOUSE STYLE

House style is the way a newspaper or magazine chooses to publish in matters of detail. Is 'realise' spelt this way or with a 'z' – and should 'spelt' be 'spelled'? How is the date written, '4 July 1776' or 'July 4 1776', and should there be a comma in the middle? Is it 'Second World War' or 'second world war' or 'World War Two' or 'World War II'? Which courtesy titles (Mr, Mrs, Miss, Ms) should be used and when? What about quote marks: single or double? And so on.

The argument for consistency is very simple. Variation that has no purpose is distracting. By keeping a consistent style in matters of detail a publication encourages readers to concentrate on *what* its writers are saying. And, of course, if there is to be a consistent style, it should be a good one.

It follows that writers and sub-editors need to know the publication's house style. The usual way of ensuring this is by means of a style book issued to staff journalists and sometimes regular freelances.

WHAT THE STYLE BOOK SHOULD COVER

Common headings in newspaper and periodical style books include:

Abbreviations
Accents (on foreign words)
Americanisms
Broadcasting
Capitals or lower case
Captions
Collective nouns (singular or plural)
Courts and legal terms
Dates
Figures
Foreign words, names and places

Government and politics
Honours, decorations, etc.
Hyphens
Initials
Italics
Jargon
Measures (including weights)
Medical
Military
Naval and shipping
Police and crime
Race (see below)
RAF and aviation
Religion
Royal family, peerage, etc.
Service ranks and their abbreviations
Spelling (for example, 'ageing/aging', 'gaol/jail', 'realise/realize', 'spelled/spelt')
Sport
Titles of books, films, etc.
Titles of courtesy
Trade names
Universities and colleges

Specialist magazines will of course cover their own fields.

A style book should always specify a particular dictionary to be consulted on points it does not cover. The *Oxford Dictionary for Writers and Editors* is often used for this purpose.

Many style books also give guidance on general points of good English and writing style; also typesetting instructions for sub-editors.

RACISM AND SEXISM

Many style books advise: report people's race only when it is relevant to the story. Guidance is often given on when to use 'black' (of a person's skin colour as opposed to 'Black' or 'Asian' or 'negro' or 'coloured').

Some style books also advise against such words as 'businessman' (prefer 'business executive'), 'foreman' (prefer 'supervisor') and 'policeman' (prefer 'police officer'). Certainly, if both men and women are covered by the reference, it is a mistake to use the male suffix '-man' (it is a mistake partly because many readers will be offended by it). But there is no consensus in journalism about how far this process should go: some publications enthusiastically adopt such words as 'chairperson' and 'spokesperson'; others would always avoid them because they are awkward and ugly.

Opposition to sexism is also one reason for the widespread adoption of the plural pronoun 'they/them' in place of 'he/him':

If anybody comes let them in.

This is both easy to say and politically correct: it is now the accepted form in most British journalism.

But opposition to sexism is also responsible for the 'Ms' complication. To avoid having to call people 'Miss' or 'Mrs' anti-sexists use the American import 'Ms' – which gives us three rival courtesy titles to choose from. A better bet surely would be to do without such titles altogether: this is already the style of many publications.

FALSE DISTINCTIONS

Style books can go too far, drawing distinctions that turn out to be false. For example, some try to distinguish between double quotes for speech and single quotes for emphasis; or between 'judgment' spelt one way for a legal decision and 'judgement' spelt another way for an ordinary opinion; or between 'inquiry' for an official investigation and 'enquiry' for an ordinary question.

This sort of thing doesn't work because it conflicts with usage: most publications use either double or single quotes for both quotation and emphasis, and use the same spelling for different uses of a word.

Occasionally, usage does make the distinction: the American (and original English) 'program' is used of computers while the French 'programme' is used of TV, concerts and everything else.

CHAPTER 8

STYLE

Style differs from grammar in that it cannot be quantified: it has no precise rules. Style is concerned not so much with the mechanics of language as with the way the writer uses it to play on the sensations of the reader. Style adds impact to writing, strengthens the contact with the reader and heightens their awareness. This is true even though the reader may be unaware of what is happening and unable to analyse the techniques used.

To be effective, a journalist must develop a style that has four principal attributes: suitability, simplicity, precision and poise.

SUITABILITY

The way a story is written must match the subject, the mood and pace of the events described and, above all, the needs of the reader. The style must arouse their interest and maintain it throughout. It must also present the facts or arguments in a way that enables the reader to understand them quickly and easily. For example:

1 If the subject is serious, treat it seriously.
2 If the subject is light, treat it lightly – for example, use a delayed-drop intro or a punning headline.
3 Whatever the subject, do not needlessly offend the reader. Thus, where a story concerns eccentric beliefs or practices, avoid cynicism and facetiousness.
4 Where a story concerns events that have action and movement, the style should suggest pace. Write tersely; avoid superfluous adjectives and adverbs; use direct, active verbs; construct crisp, taut sentences.
5 Where a story concerns a sequence of events, a straightforward narrative style may be the best bet. If you use one event to create impact in the intro, remember to repeat the reference in its proper time context. Also, make sure your tenses are consistent.
6 Where a story concerns stark, horrific events, avoid the temptation to overwrite. The events themselve will provide all the impact you need.

7 Whatever the story, don't rhapsodise. Remember that understatement is usually more effective than overstatement.

SIMPLICITY

Be direct: get to the point. For example:

1 Prefer the short, Anglo-Saxon word to the long, Latinate one.
2 Prefer the concrete statement to the abstract one.
3 Prefer the direct statement to any form of circumlocution.
4 Avoid words or phrases that merely sound good.
5 Avoid pomposity at all costs.
6 Remember that a sentence must have at least one verb – and that this is its most important word.
7 In general, use transitive verbs in the active voice:

Jones told the meeting he was resigning.

8 Choose adjectives with care and don't use too many. Avoid tautology: 'a *new* innovation'.
9 In general, prefer the short sentence to the long one, particularly in the intro.
10 Avoid over-complex sentences full of subordinate clauses and phrases.

PRECISION

Precision is vital to the journalist, above all in news reporting. To be precise you need to know exactly what words mean. Study words and their meanings and never use a word you are not sure about. Read Chapter 9, *Words*, carefully and then refer to it when necessary.

You must also master the principles of grammar to ensure that you express your meaning clearly and accurately. Read the chapters on grammar carefully and then refer to them when necessary.

As a writer, do not leave it to the sub to spot inaccuracy or ambiguity. Read your own copy and ask: 'Do I mean what I say and have I said what I mean?' Often the honest answer will be: 'No.'

If you pass that self-imposed test, ask: 'So what?' Often you will find that the story does not go far enough in saying what happens next. Remember that the reader needs to know precisely what is happening.

As a sub, always check when you rewrite that you haven't introduced new errors into the copy. And be careful when you write news headlines to fit. If your first effort is the wrong length, you will try to substitute one word for another. But a synonym must be exact or it may change the meaning of the headline. Always ask yourself finally: 'Does the headline tell the story?' If the answer is 'No', it will need further rewriting.

Also, be careful with verbs where the active and passive voice take the same form:

PEER OWED £20,000

This is ambiguous: was he owed the money or did he owe it?

POISE

Poise is the essence of style: it gives writing balance, ease of manner and lack of strain. Individual words should fit the context. Sentences should be a pleasure to read because they are balanced and rhythmical. Paragraphs should be written to convey the writer's meaning and leave the reader in no doubt that they have grasped it.

With the best prose the reader remains unconscious of technique: they simply enjoy reading the passage. The hard work should all be done by the writer (with a bit of polish by the sub).

Study the section on stylistic devices that follows. Practise using them where appropriate. But, above all, look for good models in journalism and writing generally. If a piece of prose excites you, study it, analyse it – even imitate it. Do not be too proud to copy other writers' tricks.

STYLISTIC DEVICES

Most of the stylistic devices that follow are called tropes or figures of speech. There is no reason why you should learn the names of the more obscure ones, such as synecdoche or metonymy. But the curious thing is that we take both of these for granted. What could be more natural than to say 'All hands on deck' (synecdoche) or 'He is a lover of the bottle' (metonymy)? But it is worth remembering that they are in fact figures of speech.

ALLITERATION

Alliteration is the repetition of an initial sound in words that follow each other:

Sing a song of sixpence

Use in light-hearted stories, particularly in headlines. Do not use in serious stories.

ASSONANCE

Assonance is the repetition of a vowel sound in words that follow each other:

The cat sat on my lap.

Use in light-hearted stories, particularly in headlines. Do not use in serious stories.

GRAVEYARD (ALSO BLACK, GALLOWS, SICK) HUMOUR

This is making jokes about such things as injury, disease, disability and death. It is an understandable reaction by journalists (also police officers, soldiers, doctors, nurses and others) to the hard facts of life and death.

Enjoy the jokes but do not let them get into print. The headline 'Hot under the cholera' once appeared over a story about an epidemic. This is also an example of the compulsive pun.

HYPERBOLE

Hyperbole is extravagant and obvious exaggeration:

a million thanks

Of all figures of speech, hyperbole is the most used – and abused – by journalists. So the message must be: handle with care.

IRONY

Irony is either making a point in words that literally mean the opposite or a condition in which a person seems mocked by fate or the facts.

A story about a woman who survives a car crash, borrows a mobile phone and telephones her husband to report her survival – only to be knocked down and killed a moment later – is an example of irony.

In this example telling the story is enough: we do not need to be reminded that it is irony.

Use the word 'irony' sparingly. In particular, avoid the adverb 'ironically' which is usually a lazy way of trying to make a surprise sound more significant than it is.

LITOTES

Litotes is the opposite of hyperbole. It is understatement, especially assertion by negation of the contrary. Instead of 'Rome is a great city':

Rome is no mean city.

METAPHOR

Metaphor is calling something by the name of what it resembles:

To suffer the slings and arrows of outrageous fortune

Frequent repetition of metaphors turns them into clichés (see Chapter 9, *Words*). Careless use of metaphors can lead to the mixed metaphor, an expression in which two or more metaphors are confused:

to take arms against a sea of troubles
(you wouldn't use *weapons* to fight the *waves*)

The fact that Shakespeare did it is no defence: Hamlet was mad. So avoid the mixed metaphor at all costs since it has the opposite effect of that intended. Instead of making your prose vivid it produces the effect of absurdity.

METONYMY

Metonymy is replacing the name of something by the name of a related thing:

He is a lover of the bottle [instead of drink].

ONOMATOPOEIA

Onomatopoeia is using words whose sound helps to suggest the meaning:

He has a hacking cough.

OXYMORON

Oxymoron is combining contradictory terms to form an expressive phrase:

He shows cruel kindness.

PUN

A pun is a play on words alike or nearly alike in sound but different in meaning:

ALL THE FAX ABOUT NEW TECHNOLOGY

The pun is overused by headline-writers who can't break the habit. *Never use a pun over a serious story.*

A subtler form of word play recycles an old meaning:

ARE YOU A VIRGIN ABOUT OLIVE OIL?

REPETITION

Repetition on purpose emphasises:

Romeo, Romeo; wherefore art thou Romeo?

In general, prefer repetition to variation.

RHETORIC

Rhetoric is a general term for the art of using language to persuade or impress others. Note particularly the rhetorical question that journalists address to their readers:

Have you ever been to China?

Use in chatty features, but rarely elsewhere.

SIMILE

Simile is likening something to something else:

My love is like a red, red rose

Frequent repetition of similes turn them into clichés (see Chapter 9, *Words*) – avoid them like the plague.

SYNECDOCHE

Synecdoche is using the part for the whole or the whole for the part:

All hands on deck.

VARIATION

Variation is using a different word or phrase to describe something in order to avoid repetition and/or to add colour to the copy. When done to impress it is called 'elegant variation':

Instead of talking about *a spade* I shall from now on refer to *a horticultural implement.*

This kind of variation is a bad idea because what results is at least strained and sometimes ludicrous.

More common is the variation that tries to avoid repetition:

Northern Ireland has a higher rate of unemployment than at any other time in *the province's* history.

Before using this kind of variation ask yourself the following questions:

1 Would a pronoun do as well? In the example above 'its' could easily replace 'the province's'.
2 Is the variation word/phrase an exact equivalent? (Here the province of Ulster has three counties in the Irish Republic.)
3 Is the variation necessary or could you avoid it by rewriting the sentence?
4 Would repetition have as much impact as variation?

The need to repeat or vary words is often a clue to bad structure. For example, where an intro doubles back on itself, it should be rewritten. Where you are tempted to use 'however' because you have just used 'but', you are making the reader work too hard.

CHAPTER 9

WORDS

Precision and effectiveness in writing depend on the careful use of language. You must learn to recognise the words and phrases that will convey your meaning exactly and vividly to the reader. And you must reject any word or phrase that is flabby and worn out.

The development of word power comes only with practice. Besides a sensitivity to language it demands an inquiring mind and a careful attitude. You must avoid careless mistakes and also be concerned about quality, taking professional pride in your skill as a writer.

This attitude cannot be taught, only caught. But it is worth pointing out common pitfalls.

EXAGGERATION

Many errors occur because the writer overstates the case in an effort to achieve impact: this is perhaps the journalist's most common fault. It is this striving for effect that makes every rescuer 'a hero', every disturbance a 'fracas', every confusion a 'chaos' and every fire an 'inferno' (the word means hell).

Here the advice must be: never use a word whose meaning you are unsure about; always check the dictionary definition and derivation of an unfamiliar word.

TABLOIDESE

The search for a short word to use in a headline has created a specialised subs' vocabulary that, on some papers, turns every investigation into a 'probe', every attempt into a 'bid' and every disagreement into a 'row'. It would be perverse to object to the use of these words in headlines, although a succession of them reads like parody. A sub who writes:

VICE VICAR TELLS ALL IN PROBE BID ROW

is clearly overdoing it.

The real problem comes when this essentially made-up language creeps into the text. Such words as 'rap', 'slam' and 'axe' litter the pages of the downmarket tabloids. As Keith Waterhouse has pointed out, the objection to these words is that people don't use them in everyday speech.

> *Why, if these words are now so common, are they not in common use?*
> *Why do we not hear housewives at bus-stops saying . . . 'Did I tell you*
> *about young Fred being rapped after he slammed his boss? He thinks he's*
> *going to be axed'?* (Keith Waterhouse, *Waterhouse on Newspaper Style*,
> Viking, 1989 pp229–30)

So think hard before using the following words in text:

aid	(for help)
aim	(intend)
alert	(tell)
axe	(sack)
ban	(prohibit, exclude)
bar	(exclude)
battle	(dispute)
bid	(try, attempt)
blast	(criticise)
blaze	(fire)
blitz	(drive)
blow	(disappointment)
blunder	(mistake)
bombshell	(unexpected event)
boob	(mistake, breast)
boost	(encourage, increase)
boot out	(expel)
brand	(describe)
bungle	(mistake)
call	(propose)
chief	(leader)
clampdown	(control)
clash	(dispute)
condemn	(criticise)
crackdown	(control)
crusade	(campaign)
curb	(restrict)
curse	(bad luck)

dash	(hurry)
deal	(agreement, arrangement)
don	(put on)
drama	(event)
dramatic	(unusual)
dub	(describe)
dump	(sack)
dwell	(live)
epic	(very unusual)
face	(expect)
feud	(quarrel)
fury	(anger)
grab	(take)
headache	(problem)
hike	(increase)
hit out	(criticise)
hurdle	(difficulty)
inferno	(fire)
jinx	(bad luck)
kick out	(expel)
launch	(start)
loom	(threaten)
mercy	(relief)
oust	(replace)
outrage	(anger)
peace	(end to dispute)
plan	(proposal)
pledge	(promise)
plunge	(fall)
poised	(ready)
probe	(inquiry)
quit	(resign)

quiz	(question)
race	(hurry)
rally	(support)
rap	(rebuke)
rebel	(person disagreeing)
riddle	(mystery)
rock	(shock)
romp	(sex, have sex)
row	(dispute)
rumpus	(dispute)
scrap	(cancel)
set to	(likely to)
shake-up	(reform)
shock	(surprise)
shun	(avoid)
slam	(criticise)
slap	(impose)
slash	(reduce)
snag	(difficulty)
snub	(fail to attend)
soar	(increase)
storm out	(resign)
swoop	(raid)
threat	(possibility)
unveil	(announce)
vice	(sex)
vigil	(patrol)
vow	(promise)
war	(rivalry)

POSH WORDS

Posh, pompous, pretentious words are the opposite of tabloidese: they show the writer putting on collar and tie to impress. Many posh words used in journalism are also examples of circumlocution (long-winded and round-about writing) or euphemism (using a mild-sounding alternative word to avoid giving offence). In general, prefer plain words to posh ones. For example, avoid:

a large proportion of	(use much of)
accede to	(allow, grant)
accommodate	(hold)
accordingly	(so)
additionally	(also)
adjacent to	(near, next to)
ameliorate	(improve)
amidst	(amid)
amongst	(among)
approximately	(about)
ascertain	(learn)
assist/ance	(help)
at an early date	(soon)
at present/at the present time	(now)
attempt	(try)
beverage	(drink)
commence	(begin, start)
concept	(idea)
concerning	(about)
construct	(build, make)
converse	(talk)
customary	(usual)
deceased	(dead)
demise	(death)
demonstrate	(show)
dentures	(false teeth)
despite	(although)
discontinue	(stop)
dispatch	(send)
donate	(give)
draw to the attention of	(point out)
dwell	(live)
edifice	(building)
endeavour	(try)
eventuate	(happen)
evince	(show)
exceedingly	(very)

expedite	(hurry)
extremely	(very)
facilitate	(ease, help)
finalise	(complete)
following	(after)
frequently	(often)
give rise to	(cause)
implement	(carry out)
in addition	(also)
in addition to	(as well as)
in attendance	(present)
in conjunction with	(and)
in consequence of	(because)
indicate	(show, point, point out, say, imply)
in excess of	(more than)
inform	(tell)
initiate	(begin, start)
in order to	(to)
inquire	(ask)
in short supply	(scarce)
in spite of the fact that	(although)
in the course of	(during)
in the event of	(if)
in the neighbourhood/vicinity of	(near)
in the region of	(about)
in view of the fact that	(since)
less expensive	(cheaper)
locate	(find)
location	(place)
made good their escape	(escaped)
manufacture	(make)
missive	(letter)
necessitate	(compel)
nevertheless	(but)
nonetheless	(but)
objective	(aim)
of the order of	(about)
on the part of	(by)
owing to the fact that	(because)

pass away/over/to the other side	(die)
personnel	(workers)
previous	(earlier)
prior to	(before)
proceed	(go)
purchase	(buy)
regarding	(about)
remunerate	(pay)
require	(need)
residence	(home)
resuscitate	(revive)
somewhat	(rather)
subsequently	(later)
sufficient	(enough)
terminate	(end)
to date	(so far)
transportation	(transport)
upon	(on)
utilise	(use)
venue	(place)
was of the opinion that	(thought)
was suffering from	(had)
when and if	(if)
whilst	(while)
with the exception of	(except)

The word 'dwell' contrives to be both tabloidese and posh: a double reason for not using it. The word 'indicate' is a particular trap: does it mean show, point, point out, say or imply? If it's precision you want, avoid 'indicate' altogether.

VOGUE WORDS

Some (usually long) words become fashionable. Suddenly they are everywhere – used with meaningless frequency by journalists who are keen to be considered smart or who are too idle to develop their own vocabulary.

Using a phrase such as 'the eponymous protagonist' to describe Hamlet is almost always a sign of showing off. So take care with the following:

agenda	insulate
ambience	
ambivalent	meaningful
archetypal	meritocracy
axiomatic	milieu
	mores
cachet	
catalyst	parameter
charisma	pragmatism
conceptual	protagonist
coterie	purposive
dichotomy	replete
dilemma	
	seminal
egregious	symbiosis
emotive	syndrome
empathy	
eponymous	technocrat
escalate	
exponential	vertiginous
	viable
iconic	vicarious

If you are tempted to use one of these words ask yourself:

1 Is it the exact word you need?
2 Is there an alternative that would be as accurate – and more comprehensible?
3 If not, can the word be understood from its context, or does it need some qualification to help the reader? (If it does then perhaps it is not the right word.)

JARGON

Jargon is specialised vocabulary, familiar to the members of a group, trade or profession. If you write for a newspaper or general magazine you should try to translate jargon into ordinary English whenever you can. If you write for a specialist magazine there is a stronger case for leaving some terms as they are, but you must be sure that the reader will understand them.

A common source of jargon is scientific, medical, government and legal handouts. Avoid such examples of officialese as:

ambulatory patient	(for one that has been allowed up)
domiciliary unit	(home)
hospitalised	(sent to hospital)

There are also ugly words in industry, but you cannot always avoid them. 'Containerisation', for example, has a precise meaning and is difficult to translate.

'Redundancy' may appear to be a euphemism for sacking – but there is a big difference between the two terms. A person made redundant will not be replaced: their job has been abolished. A person sacked is likely to be replaced.

'Packing' is not the same as 'packaging'; 'marketing' is not the same as 'selling'; 'targeting' may be an ugly word but it is what sales and marketing people say they do when they set out to identify and capture a market. So use these terms where necessary in context but do not use them in general stories.

The computer industry has spawned its own ugly terminology – answer-back, boot up, end-user, formatted, throughput, input, hardware, software. It is apt for that industry since it conveys particular, precise meanings to those who work with computers.

But journalists (except those on computer magazines) should avoid such terms as 'throughput'. We already have words to describe these ideas. They may be less trendy but they are at least as clear as computer jargon and certainly more elegant.

SLANG

Slang is the jargon of the street – and similar arguments apply to it. Does the reader understand it? Is it ugly? Has the word become accepted?

And does it fit the context? You would not use slang in reporting the mayor's funeral – but you might well use jazz slang in writing a colour piece on Dizzy Gillespie's funeral.

Use with care.

WORDS WITH TWO MEANINGS

With some words the problem is that they mean different things to different people. To the history don, for example, a '*chauvinist*' is an aggressive patriot, a flag-waver, while to almost anyone under 40 a chauvinist is somebody who puts women down.

Below are some examples of words that can cause confusion. So use them with care – if in doubt, find an alternative.

Note: in each case the first meaning given is the earlier, 'correct' one, even though the later, looser one may now be more common. (See also *Confusing pairs*, below.)

aggravate: 1 make worse; 2 annoy
alibi: 1 defence to a charge based on being able to prove that you were somewhere else when a crime was being committed; 2 excuse
anticipate: 1 use, spend, deal with in advance; 2 expect
arguably: 1 possibly; 2 probably
celibate: 1 unmarried; 2 abstaining from sex
chauvinist: 1 absurdly nationalistic; 2 sexist
chronic: 1 lingering, recurrent; 2 very bad, severe
cohort: 1 group of people (originally military); 2 individual colleague or assistant
contemporary: 1 belonging to the same time; 2 modern
decimate: 1 kill one in ten; 2 kill or destroy large numbers
dilemma: 1 choice between two equally unwelcome possibilities; 2 awkward problem
fulsome: 1 excessive; 2 copious
gay: 1 light-hearted; 2 homosexual
geriatric: 1 relating to care of the old; 2 old
ilk: 1 same (as in 'of that ilk'); 2 family, class or set
pristine: 1 original, former; 2 new, fresh, pure
protagonist: 1 chief actor; 2 any participant
refute: 1 show to be false; 2 contradict, deny
regularly: 1 at regular intervals; 2 often
shambles: 1 slaughterhouse; 2 confusion

CONFUSING PAIRS

There are many pairs of words in English that sound similar and are often confused. The pitfall here is not that the two words are thought to have the same meaning but that the unwary writer uses one by mistake for the other – and thus produces an entirely different meaning. In some cases (such as the trio 'assure/ensure/insure') each word has gradually acquired its own distinct meaning: they all mean 'make sure' but in different ways.

See also Chapter 4, *Spelling*, for pairs of words that sound identical and are often confused.

abrogate (abolish)/arrogate (claim presumptiously)
affect (influence, adopt)/effect (as verb, accomplish)
appraise (determine the value of)/apprise (inform)
assure (give confidence to)/ensure (make happen)/insure (arrange insurance)

barbaric (crude, uncivilised)/barbarous (cruel)

censor (prevent publication)/censure (criticise harshly)
chafe (make sore)/chaff (tease)
complacent (smug)/complaisant (obliging)
contemptible (deserving contempt)/contemptuous (showing contempt)
continual (recurring with breaks)/continuous (without a break)
credible (believable)/credulous (believing too easily)

defective (damaged)/deficient (short of)
definite (precise)/definitive (conclusive)
deprecate (argue or protest against)/depreciate (fall in value)
derisive (showing contempt)/derisory (deserving contempt)
disinterested (impartial)/uninterested (bored)

economic (of economics, enough to give a good return)/economical (thrifty)
elemental (basic)/elementary (simple)
equable (steady)/equitable (fair)
evolve (develop)/devolve (hand down)
exigent (urgent)/exiguous (scanty)
explicit (stated in detail)/implicit (implied)

farther (used of distance only)/further (used of quantity and distance)
flaunt (display ostentatiously)/flout (treat with contempt)
forceful (energetic)/forcible (done by force)

historic (famous in history)/historical (belonging to history)

imply (suggest)/infer (conclude)
ingenious (cleverly contrived)/ingenuous (frank)
intense (extreme)/intensive (concentrated)

luxuriant (profuse)/luxurious (expensive)

masterful (dominating)/masterly (skilful)
militate (contend)/mitigate (soften)

oral (spoken)/verbal (of words, written or spoken)

ordinance (decree)/ordnance (arrangement, usually military)

partly (in part)/partially (incompletely)
politic (prudent)/political (of politics)
prescribe (lay down)/proscribe (prohibit)
prevaricate (evade the truth)/procrastinate (defer action)

repel (offend)/repulse (drive back)

sensual (physical, gratifying to the body)/sensuous (affecting or appeal-
ing to the senses, especially by beauty or delicacy)

venal (corruptible)/venial (excusable)

REDUNDANT WORDS

Many words used are superfluous, for example adjectives ('*true* facts'),
prepositions ('fill *up* a bottle') or phrases ('for *the month of* January').
Often a writer feels the need to add a redundant word or phrase because
they do not know the meaning of a particular word. Never do this. Always
check what a word means, then decide whether your reader will understand it – without the redundant addition. Here are some examples to
avoid:

appreciate *in value*
chief protagonist
close scrutiny
completely surround
comprise *of*
consensus *of opinion*
general consensus
revert *back*
temporary respite
total annihilation

NON-EXISTENT WORDS

By all means make up a word if the context demands it. But avoid making
up non-existent words by mistake. Do not run together words that belong
apart or add syllables to words that do not need them. For example use:

a lot *not* alot
dissociate *not* disassociate
on to *not* onto
preventive *not* preventative

recur *not* reoccur

But 'alright' is now all right in many publications: check your house style.

EMPTY WORDS

Some words are, simply, empty. 'Simply' used like this is one of them. So is 'basically'. They tend to be used in speech as an alternative to 'er' to give the speaker thinking time. Avoid them in writing unless in quoting somebody you wish to give the impression that they are empty headed. For example:

at the end of the day
basically
by and large
currently
I mean
meaningful
simply
you know
well

FOREIGN WORDS

Many foreign words and phrases are now part of English. Indeed the flow of words from French has not stopped since the Norman invasion. As the world's most important international language, English inevitably adopts words from other languages all the time. Latin, by contrast, since it is losing ground in schools, is now recognised by fewer British people.

In general, be careful with words of foreign origin. Use them accurately but not pretentiously, always asking yourself: 'Will my reader understand this?'

If your house style includes accents, make sure that you use them consistently. For example 'paté' and 'emigré' are howlers; they should be 'pâté' and 'émigré'.

Watch your spelling of foreign words: 'de rigueur' includes the letter 'u' twice; 'restaurateur' has no 'n'; 'bête noire' has an 'e' at the end.

Do not litter your copy with words that need to be italicised because they are unfamiliar foreign words. If a word needs italics, translate it into English.

For the plurals of foreign words see Chapter 4, *Spelling*, pp27–8.

AMERICANISMS

American is not a foreign language but a dialect (or series of dialects) of English. And to it we owe much of the vigour of modern English prose. Without writers such as Hemingway our language would be a tired, anaemic thing. But many of the Americanisms that have become current are ugly, pointless and should be avoided. For example, do not use:

to consult with	(for to consult)
to gift	(to give)
to loan	(to lend)
transportation	(transport)
utilisation	(use)

CLICHÉS

Everybody who advises on writing in general and journalism in particular says you must avoid clichés. And you must certainly try to avoid the hilarious/embarrassing ones listed below. But a certain amount of formula-writing, both in structure and vocabulary, is inevitable in routine journalism, whether it is a news story or a piece of instructional copy. A worse fault is to try so hard to be original that you end up sounding pretentious.

And there is of course a worse mistake than using a cliché: misusing one. Do not write 'He is as deaf as a doornail' or 'She is as dead as a post.' Avoid mixing two clichés together. Do not write: 'I am full of nothing but praise.' This runs together into a nonsensical cocktail the two stock phrases 'I am full of (praise)' and 'I have nothing but (praise).'

The following list of clichés appeared in *A Journalist's Guide to the Use of English* published in 1971:

acid test	clutches of the law
any shape or form	cool as a cucumber
	crying need
beggars description	
bitter end	dame fashion
blow by blow	dark horse
breakthrough	dastardly deed
bring to a head	dead as a dodo
burning issue	deaf as a post
	denizens of the deep
cheer to the echo	down under
city fathers	

each and every
extra special

face up to
fair means or foul
fair sex
fan the flames
fast and loose
flash in the pan
foregone conclusion

goes without saying
golden handshake
great beyond
grim reaper

high dudgeon
horns of a dilemma

interesting to note

jet-propelled

last but not least
leave no stone unturned

like rats in a trap
limped into port
long years
loom up

monotous regularity

news leaked out

out and about

pillar of the establishment
pool of blood

red letter day

sea of faces
speculation was rife

take the bull by the horns
theory exploded
this day and age
this point in time
true facts
turned turtle

MISQUOTATIONS AND MISTAKES

Journalists should know what they are talking about. And when they quote, whether it is the people they interview or the books they read, they should quote accurately. For example, it isn't 'a little knowledge' that is said to be a dangerous thing but 'a little learning'. So also:

All that *glisters* [not 'glitters'] is not gold.
To gild refined gold, to paint the lily [not 'to gild the lily'].
Till death *us do* [not 'do us'] part.
Water, water everywhere *nor any* [not 'and not a'] drop to drink.
The 'mother of Parliaments' is not the House of Commons but England.

And Humphrey Bogart in *Casablanca* never says: 'Play it again, Sam.'

Similarly, there are some common expressions that are almost always misused. For example, 'to beg the question' does not mean 'to raise the question' but to avoid the question and so to use as the basis of proof something that itself needs proving. It means arguing in a circle.

'The exception proves the rule' means that the exception tests the rule (from the original meaning of 'prove' which also gives us the page proof and that other phrase 'the proof of the pudding is in the eating'), and in law that the making of an exception proves that the rule holds *in cases not excepted* (a notice saying 'Today students may leave early' implies that they usually have to stay late). The expression cannot mean that an exception to the rule makes it valid.

And finally journalists almost always get the King Canute story wrong. When he told the tide to stop coming in he was not arrogantly expecting it to obey him; by contrast he was showing his courtiers that he was not omnipotent.

Here, as everywhere, the moral is: if you want to be sure, get hold of a reference book and check.

GLOSSARY OF TERMS USED IN JOURNALISM

ascender: portion of lower-case letter that sticks out above the x-height

bleed: (of an image) go beyond the type area to the edge of the page
blurb: another name for standfirst or similar displayed copy
body type: the main typeface in which a story is set
bold: thick black type used for emphasis
broadsheet: large-format newspaper such as the *Times*
bust (to): (of a headline) be too long for the space available
byline: name of journalist who has written the story

caps: capital letters
cast off (to): estimate length of copy
centre (to): set (headline) with equal space on either side
centre spread: middle opening of tabloid or magazine
chapel: office branch of media union
character: unit of measurement for type including letters, figures, punctuation marks and spaces
chief sub: senior journalist in charge of sub-editors
colour piece: news story written as feature with emphasis on journalist's reactions
copy: text of story
crosshead: occasional line(s) of type, usually bigger and bolder than body type, inserted between paragraphs to liven up page

deadline: time by which a journalist must complete story
deck: one of series of headlines stacked on top of each other
descender: portion of lower-case letter that sticks out below the x-height
delayed drop: device in news story of delaying important facts for effect
deskman: American term for male sub-editor
display type: type for headlines, etc.
double spread: two facing pages
dummy: 1 photocopied or printed (but not distributed) version of new publication used for practice and discussion; 2 blank version of estab-

lished publication, for example, to show weight of paper; 3 complete set of page proofs

edition: version of newspaper printed for particular circulation area or time

editorial: 1 leading article expressing publication's opinion; 2 matter that is not advertising

em, en: units of measurement for type – the width of the letters m and n

face: type design

feature: article that goes beyond reporting of facts to explain and/or entertain

file (to): transmit copy

flatplan: page-by-page plan of magazine issue

flush left or right: (of type) have one consistent margin with the other ragged

fount (pronounced 'font' and sometimes spelt that way): typeface

freelance: self-employed journalist who sells material to various media

freelancer: American term for freelance

full out: (of type) not indented

galley proof: typeset proof not yet made up into a page

hack: jocular term for journalist

hanging indent: set copy with first line of each paragraph full out and subsequent lines indented

heavy: broadsheet newspaper

house style: see Chapter 7

indent: set copy several characters in from left-hand margin

input (to): type copy into computer

intro: first paragraph of story

italics: italic (sloping) type

journo: jocular term for journalist

justified: type set with consistent margins

layout: arrangement of body type, headlines and illustrations on the page

leader: leading article expressing publication's opinion

leading (pronounced 'ledding'): space between lines (originally made by inserting blank slugs of lead between lines of type)

leg: column of typeset copy

legal (to): check for legal problems such as libel

lensman: American term for male photographer

literal: typographical error

lower case: ordinary letters (not caps)

make-up: assembly of type and illustrations on the page ready for printing

newsman: American term for male reporter

nib: news in brief – short news item
night lawyer: barrister who reads proofs for legal problems

op-ed: feature page facing that with leading articles

page proof: proof of a made-up page
par, para: paragraph
paste-up: page layout pasted into position
pay-off: final twist or flourish in the last paragraph of a story
pic, pix: press photograph(s)
pica: unit of type measurement
piece: article
point: 1 full stop; 2 standard unit of type size
proofread (to): check proofs
pyramid (usually inverted): conventional structure for news story with most important facts in intro

query: question mark
quote: verbatim quotation
quotes: quotation marks

range left or right: (of type) have one consistent margin with the other ragged
reverse out: reversal of black and white areas of printed image
roman: plain upright type
run on: (of type) continue from one line, column or page to the next

sanserif: plain type
screamer: exclamation mark
sell: another name for standfirst, often used in women's magazines
serif: decorative addition to type
setting: copy set in type
shy: (of headline) too short for the space available
side-head: subsidiary heading
snapper: jocular term for press photographer
snaps: press photographs
spike: where rejected copy goes
splash: tabloid's main front-page story
splash sub: sub responsible for tabloid's front page
standfirst: introductory matter, particularly used with features
stet: ignore deletion (Latin for 'let it stand')
stone sub: sub-editor who makes final corrections and cuts on page proofs
story: article, especially news report
strap(line): introductory words above main headline
Street (the): Fleet Street, where many newspapers once had their offices
stringer: freelance on contract to a news organisation

sub: sub-editor – journalist who checks, corrects, rewrites copy, writes headlines, captions, etc., and checks proofs; on newspapers, but not on most magazines, subs are also responsible for layout

tabloid: popular small-format newspaper such as the *Sun*
think piece: feature written to show and provoke thought
typo: American term for typographical error

underscore: underline
upper case: capital letters

widow: line of type consisting of a single word or syllable
wob: white on black – type reversed out

x-height: height of the lower-case letters of a typeface (excluding ascenders and descenders)

FURTHER READING*

JOURNALISM

Although the famous Harold Evans series is out of print, there are books available on most aspects of British journalism. Waterhouse is particularly well written and fun to read, and Spiegl is a laugh a line. Although it has a specialist title, Albert's book makes many useful general points.

Aitchison, James, *Writing for the Press*, Hutchinson, 1988.
Albert, Tim, *Medical Journalism*, Radcliffe Medical Press, 1992.
Bagnall, Nicholas, *Newspaper Language*, Butterworth/Heinemann, 1993.
Boyd, Andrew, *Broadcast Journalism*, Butterworth/Heinemann, 1993.
Chantler, Paul and Harris, Sam, *Local Radio Journalism*, Butterworth/ Heinemann, 1993.
Clayton, Joan, *Journalism for Beginners*, Piatkus, 1992.
Davis, Anthony, *Magazine Journalism Today*, Butterworth/Heinemann, 1988.
Dick, Jill, *Freelance Writing for Newspapers*, A. & C. Black, 1991.
Dobson, Christopher, *Freelance Journalism*, Butterworth/Heinemann, 1992.
Evans, Harold, *Newsman's English*, Heinemann, 1972, out of print. (Also by Evans in the same series: *Handling Newspaper Text*, *News Headlines*, *Picture Editing*, *Newspaper Design*, all published in 1972; all out of print.)
Giles, Vic and Hodgson, Frank, *Creative Newspaper Design*, Butterworth/ Heinemann, 1990
Goldie, Fay, *Successful Freelance Journalism*, Oxford University Press, 1985.
Greenwood, Walter and Welsh, Tom, *McNae's Essential Law for Journalists*, Butterworth, 1992.
Harris, Geoffrey and Spark, David, *Practical Newspaper Reporting*, Butterworth/Heinemann, 1993.

*Dates refer to the most recent known edition.

78

Henessy, Brendan, *Writing Feature Articles*, Butterworth/Heinemann, 1993.
Hodgson, Frank, *Subediting: Newspaper Editing and Production*, Butterworth/Heinemann, 1987.
—— *Modern Newspaper Practice*, Butterworth/Heinemann, 1992.
Hoffman, Ann, *Research for Writers*, A. & C. Black, 1992.
Hutt, Alan, and James, Bob, *Newspaper Design Today*, Lund Humphries, 1988.
Jones, Graham, *Business of Freelancing*, BFP Books, 1987.
Keene, M., *Practical Photojournalism*, Butterworth/Heinemann, 1993.
Sellers, Leslie, *The Simple Subs Book*, 2nd edn, Pergamon, 1985.
Spiegl, Fritz, *Keep Taking the Tabloids*, Pan, 1983, out of print.
—— *Media Speak/Media Write*, Elm Tree Books, 1989.
Waterhouse, Keith, *Waterhouse on Newspaper Style* (replaces *Daily Mirror Style*, now out of print), Viking, 1989.

ENGLISH USAGE AND STYLE

THE CLASSICS

On usage the standard texts are Fowler and Gowers; on style Quiller-Couch and Middleton Murry. There is also a famous essay by George Orwell and an American gem, Strunk and White.

Fowler, H. W., *The King's English*, Oxford University Press, 1931.
—— *A Dictionary of Modern English Usage*, Oxford University Press, 1983.
Gowers, Ernest, *The Complete Plain Words*, revised by Bruce Fraser, Penguin, 1987.
Murry, J. Middleton, *The Problem of Style*, Oxford University Press, 1922, out of print.
Orwell, George, 'Politics and the English Language', in Sonia Orwell and Ian Angus, eds, *Collected Essays, Journalism and Letters of George Orwell*, vol. IV, Penguin, 1970.
Quiller-Couch, Arthur, *On the Art of Writing*, Cambridge University Press, 1919, out of print.
Strunk, William and White, E. B. *The Elements of Style*, New York: Macmillan, 1979.

THE MODERNS

Many of the books listed below are by journalists. Particularly recommended are Bryson, Phythian (a distinguished school teacher) and the Chambers guide. Lanham is a spirited attack on the classics.

Bryson, Bill, *The Penguin Dictionary of Troublesome Words*, Penguin, 1984.
Crystal, David, *Who Cares about English Usage?*, Pelican, 1984.
Davidson, George W., *Pocket Guide to Good English*, Chambers, 1985.
Dummett, Michael, *Grammar and Style for Examination Candidates and Others*, Duckworth, 1993.
Fieldhouse, Harry, *Everyman's Good English Guide*, Dent, 1982, out of print.
Lanham, Richard A., *Style: An Anti-Textbook*, Yale University Press, 1973.
Partridge, Eric, *Usage and Abusage*, Penguin, 1973.
Phythian, B. A., *Concise Dictionary of Correct English* (replaces *Teach Yourself Good English* and *Teach Yourself Correct English*), Hodder & Stoughton, 1993.
Silverlight, John, *Words*, Macmillan, 1985, out of print.
Vallins, G. H., *Good English, Better English, The Best English*, Vallins, Pan, 1963, out of print.
Waterhouse, Keith, *English Our English*, Viking, 1991.
Whale, John, *Put It In Writing*, Dent, 1984.
Weiner, E. S. C. and Hawkins, J. M., *The Oxford Guide to the English Language*, Oxford University Press, 1984.
Wood, F. T., Flavell, R. H. and Flavell, L. M., *Current English Usage*, Macmillan, 1981.

PUNCTUATION

Carey, G. V., *Mind the Stop*, Penguin, 1971.
Clark, John, *English Punctuation and Hyphenation*, Harrap, 1990.
Partridge, Eric, *You Have a Point There*, Routledge, 1990.

HOUSE STYLE

Bryson, Bill, *Penguin Dictionary for Writers and Editors*, Viking, 1991.
Grimond, Joe, *The Economist Pocket Style Book*, Business Books, 1991.
Jenkins, Simon, ed., *Times Guide to English Style and Usage*, Times Books, 1992.
Macdowall, Ian (comp.), *Reuters Handbook for Journalists*, Butterworth/Heinemann, 1992.
The Oxford Dictionary for Writers and Editors, Oxford University Press, 1981.
The Oxford Writers' Dictionary (paperback version of *The Oxford Dictionary for Writers and Editors*), Oxford University Press, 1990.

DICTIONARIES AND THESAURUSES

Every journalist needs a good dictionary. Of those published by the four main publishers, Oxford University Press, Collins, Longmans and Chambers, the Chambers series is particularly popular among journalists.

A thesaurus can help you write headlines; its disadvantage is that it tends to blur distinctions between words. But there is a reference book that overcomes this disadvantage by combining the functions of dictionary and thesaurus:

Collins Concise Dictionary and Thesaurus, Collins, 1991.

DEVELOPMENT OF ENGLISH

The most erudite book is by Burchfield, formerly chief editor of the *Oxford English Dictionary*. The others are all worth reading. Howard, literary editor of the *Times*, has written several other books on English.

Burchfield, Robert, *The English Language*, Oxford University Press, 1986.
Bryson, Bill, *Mother Tongue*, Hamish Hamilton, 1990.
Crystal, David, *The English Language*, Pelican, 1990.
Howard, Philip, *The State of the Language*, Penguin, 1986.

Index